Fireflies in the Gathering Dark

Fireflies in the Gathering Dark

Poems by

Maril Crabtree

Kelsay Books

Cover art: (Xentape@flickr)

ISBN:13- 978-1-945752-82-7

Kelsay Books
Aldrich Press
www.kelsaybooks.com

To Virginia Lenore Briand Crabtree (1915–2014)
whose gift of avid listening the world misses
and to my beloved Jim

Acknowledgments

The root word for "inspire" comes from the Latin word *inspirare*, to breathe into. My deep thanks to all those who have lived and breathed poetry with me and inspired me to dig deeper and fly higher. Thanks especially to the Tuesday Poets (Catherine Anderson, Susan Carman, Robert Cole, Carolyn Hoppe, Mary Silwance, and Linda Tobaben); the Kansas City Writers Group, Deborah Shouse, Susan Peters, Anne Wickliffe and Jan Duncan-O'Neal; and to Leslie Ullman and Sandra Marchetti, whose encouragement and editing suggestions inspired me to keep working.

Grateful acknowledgment is made to the following publications where these poems or previous versions of them first appeared:

All Roads Will Lead You Home: "A Blessing of Wet Earth," "In the Dark"
Dead Mule School of Southern Literature: "Untamed"
The DMQ Review: "Lotus"
Earth's Daughters: "Cutting Trees"
I Am Becoming the Woman I've Wanted: "Living the Green Life"
I-70 Review: "A Mystery"
Imagination & Place/Weather: "Crossing Puget Ridge"
Kansas Roots: "A Testimony of Western Kansas Hamlets"
Kansas Time + Place: "Coming Home on the Freeway"
Literary Mama: "Mother-Daughter Conversation"
Main Street Rag: "LGBTQIA and Counting," "Stone Mermaid"
The New Laurel Review: "Blue Velvet"
Persimmon Tree: "Things to Do in the Belly of the Poem"
Potpourri: "Kairos," "Souvenir," "Journey"
Red Eft Review: "Light Confession"
Spank the Carp: "Protector"
Steam Ticket: "Moving On"
The Same: "Internal Apologia"

Up Against the Wall, Mother: "Last Illness"
Well-Versed: "The Language of Graves," "Time Piece," "In the
  Garden"

The following poems were also published in previous chapbooks:

Dancing with Elvis: "Assignation," "Living the Green Life"
Moving On: "Lotus," "Moving On," "Advice to Myself on a
  Summer Morning"
Tying the Light: "Stone Mermaid, "Crossing Puget Ridge"

Contents

III. Wild Heart

I. Remembering

Irish Lullaby for the End of the World

In honor of Hawks Well Theater, Sligo

When the last of the stars winks out
when time's constant hum falls silent
with the last breath of midnight

we'll pipe the old tunes and whistle the jigs
fingers will snap and brogues will click
and we'll find each other in the dark

In My Mother's House

Stacked ceiling high,
boxes neatly labeled:
quilt scraps, old clothes, tablecloths.
Everything has its place.
It's as if she believes
that as long as her shelves
are full,
she won't die.

Meanwhile, I try
to sort things out. I bring home
bowls—four little ones, one big one –
things I don't need
and don't want.
Nevertheless, it's five
fewer things in her house
and five more in mine.

Before I die
may my rooms be empty,
picked clean as old bones.
May I have the courage
to wear last year's dresses,
find comfort in old
books, let go, let go, and say
a clear goodbye.

Summer Back Then

Window screens, crickets, the rusty smell
of sunrisen dew, polka-dots and seersucker,
white eyelet blouses tucked into circle
skirts, ruffled swimsuits

and bologna sandwiches, wax paper-wrapped.
The nights long and steamy. We couldn't
get cool enough even with fans: floor fans,
window fans, attic fans. When we went

outside, mosquitoes chewed our flesh,
buzz-sawing our ears. They pounced and pricked
every half-inch of uncovered skin
and owned the whole outdoors. My mother wore

my father's long-sleeved shirt and khaki
workpants to hang the wash. Still, she returned
with red welts, slapping at hands and hips
as she slipped inside. What saved us, we thought,

was a truck filled with the blessed fog of DDT
that rolled across streets, through ditches, into yards.
The fogger is coming! We screamed, and our parents
shooed us inside. For awhile we had respite

from bites and whines. Until the next rains came,
when mosquitoes bloomed again.

Blue Velvet

For David

I wore a circle skirt, a scoop neck blouse.
Summer steamed outside.

In a basement of swaying teenage bodies
the 45's punched lyrics straight into my gut.

When we danced your arms circled me.
My cheek touched yours.

The rest of my body found its way
onto your red plaid shirt, your wrinkled jeans.

When we said goodnight you drove to the end
of your life.

A tangle of blood, the damp smell
of Lake Pontchartrain.

Still, when I hear that song I wish
I'd have let you kiss me.

Souvenir

The long narrow box lay in the attic next to the Christmas lights. Once, when I was ten, I asked my father what was in it. War souvenirs, he said. He took out the rifle and showed me the bayonet, how it fit onto the barrel. He plucked out a pocket-sized notebook filled with strange writing and a pack of cigarettes, cellophane broken open. I sniffed. Stale tobacco. Where did you get these? I asked. Off the body of a dead Jap, he said. He cradled the pack in his hands. *Did you kill him? Was he smoking? Writing in his notebook? Did he carry pictures of his children?* I wanted to ask but didn't. Years later when my father died, he lay in a long narrow box on a mausoleum shelf. What happened to the gun, the notebook and the cigarettes? I wanted to put them next to my father's body, send him floating across the River Styx into the next world where he could return them with apologies for stealing more than the life he was authorized to take.

Stone Mermaid

Invisible most of the time,
only when the water sinks low

does her curved tail emerge.
Waves slap her stone fins,

dark and wet. They shimmer
for an instant as if real,

as if she could escape the rock
she's anchored to once and for all.

When he came into her room
the curtains stirred. The sun slapped

its morning light against her young
cheeks, but she stood still as stone

pretending to be invisible,
underwater, the hands that brushed

over her mere minnows flowing past.
Her nightgown fluttered like a ship's

SOS as it lifted, drifted away
from childhood's safe harbor.

Remembering

How at age twelve
the world felt thick
with possibility, shelves
cluttered with budding wishes,

everything plowed
with a prickly sense
of urgency, endowed
with *if only* and *when.*

Now the air thins out
as it does when one
veers close as clouds
to the mountaintop.

Harder to see
what is unknown,
still teeming,
swollen with hope.

Things to Do in the Belly of the Poem

after *Things to Do in the Belly of the Whale* by Dan Albergotti

Count the syllables. Test the meter. Decide
on line length and stanzas: couplets, triplets,
quatrains; free verse, blank verse, formal.
In the next draft, do it all over again.

Breathe. Bake some bread. Make soup.
Take a pair of scissors to the words, cut
them apart, throw them into the air
and watch them float down. If they survive

the flight, shuffle them, change tenses, hang them
inside out and upside down. Take a yoga break
and hang your body upside down. Let the fresh
blood rush into your head and hope all the words

rearrange themselves. Breathe. Listen to Bob Dylan
and Eric Clapton. Listen to the silence between words.
Quash the longing to watch "Breaking Bad"
for the third time. Breathe. Quell the impulse to call

your best friend, your old boyfriend, the contest judge
who gave your poem first place three years ago.
Take a walk in the park. Stare at the trees and try,
really try, not to describe them in your mind. Instead,

watch the children sliding and swinging, invisible
wings halo-ing their shoulders, laughter drowning
the air. Breathe. Remember what it was like
to drift up to the clouds and sink to the bottom of time.

Unvarnished

for Barbara Robinette Moss, 1954-2009

How dare you die young, so many words
unwritten, dreams undreamed? Still, I confess

how grateful I am that you streaked into my life –
bright comet of Southern outspokenness

with an outrageous sense of living
as pure adventure. We cheered each other on.

We were two Deep South liberals
parting the waters in a red-state sea.

You laughed at death and Republicans
as you scarfed down Cajun-spiced

shrimp, fried oysters, and dirty rice.
You had no patience for injustice

or the cancer that carpeted your insides.
You didn't hide the fight against both.

You allowed hope to inhabit your days.
Best of all, you were no saint. Under the table

your toes blazed red, but you didn't hesitate
to display clay feet and embrace your failings.

Wherever your spirit hovers
I smell shrimp and nail polish, and feel loved.

Mother-Daughter Conversation

She calls from a thousand
    miles away. Instead of wandering
through our usual thickets
    of *hello-how-are-you-how-is-your-life*
our voices sound light and clear,
    without the dim static
of doubt and hesitation.
    We ride our telephone horses
toward each other, not stumbling,
    not having to dismount and look
for another way in, and she says
    you've always been my model
for feminism, for justice; now
    you're my model for compassion
and I can only pause and say
    thank you, recalling the tough survival days
and the love that rode through
    so many years to arrive, finally, here.

A Mystery

how mangroves manage to propagate
or even stay alive

with their stilt-roots walking through air
how they secrete salt

through leaf-pores leaving more room
to breathe while we

sweat out our love skin-slicked and breathless
sucking in, churning out

under the moon's indifferent glow, lying
next to the ocean's clamor

digging our souls, toes, fingernails into each other
to prove we still exist

even as the mangroves let go, die out
all over the coastal world

Last Illness

hospital corridors
call in the doctors
is she or is she not dying
mother o mother o mother

try to decide
what is real who is right
where is healing
mother o mother o mother

offer up prayers
to doctors   to God
to the gluttonous gods
of treatments and tests
mother o mother o mother

food we can bring
favorite things she can eat
must be strong to fight cancer
mother o mother o mother

comforts we bring
well-wishers   gift-givers
smile   must have hope
mother o mother o mother

killing her now not just
the cancer but doctors
and testing   blood-letting
mother o mother o mother

pricking and needling

jamming more tubes down
her throat/up her flattened blue veins
mother o mother o mother

now bring no food
too weak to eat
no need for gifts
grab for the oxygen

mother o mother o mother
no mother no mother no mother
no more

A Testimony of Western Kansas Hamlets

Thick-limbed
sturdy-tongued
the young
thoroughly churched

in elders' ways
but not afraid
to add their own.
Midwestern gesture

of two-fingered hand waves
from passing trucks
gaze squinting
against an open sun.

Coffee. Plaid shirts
with pockets. Jeans
that still huddle close
to the waist.

Socks in all seasons.
Wind and dust
play their perpetual
tunes, piano of brown

and gold keys in
a flatland orchestra
of wheat and cottonwoods
conducted in God's time.

Moving On

Along what used to be tracks
of the Union Pacific
where wheat-laden rail cars
passed several times a day
the prairie towns shine empty.
Grain bins and silos glint hollow
in the setting sun. No one
remains to tend deserted
buildings, crumbling
sidewalks, and parks where
weeds, not children, grow.
Tractors and combines rust in sheds.
Limestone fence posts
still guard ghosts of cattle herds.
Stiffened oil rigs hang black
against the sky.

Only a withered peace remains.
The soil's played out. The oil
is gone, the water's going.
The land will stay.

Internal Apologia

I'm sorry I can't remember your name.
I keep wanting to call you Paul. But I don't think
I actually know a Paul. Let's see,
there was Paul Anka—is he still around?
and Jean Paul Sartre—he definitely isn't.
Of course, I don't really know them
except in my mind. My mind is a tumbledown
cavern of shifting names, masses of words dripping
from lifetimes of files, songs from the 50's to the 90's
and beyond, nursery rhymes and church camp rounds
white coral bells upon a slender stalk
and college ditties *O it's gin, gin, gin that makes you want to sin*
words tall and dignified—*carillon* and *columnar*—
marching near words that dance all over the place
carom and *copulate* and words like *effervescence*
that spin through my brain like an old ferris wheel.
Now swoop back to names.
No, you're not Paul, you're more like a Richard or Robert.
Might as well start at the top. Andrew? Alan? Ah, lucky me -)

"Alan, so nice to see you again. How are things?"

A Fond Bon Voyage

As if she were sailing on the QE II
or on some mystic journey across the Styx,
they gathered around her open casket
to wish her farewell.

They gazed at her still face, wondering
aloud if she'd known she was dying,
if she knew when they told the doctors
to "pull the plug."

They told each other how glad they were
that she could donate her liver and kidneys
though she smoked three packs a day
and was overweight.

She loved her grandkids, though,
and the nine-year-old placed a card
full of hand-drawn butterflies
where it rested next to the Marlboros

someone else slipped in. Wherever
she went, they agreed, she'd have with her
the things she loved most.

Time Piece

time is a breaking wave

Family vacation, Pensacola Beach. Waves roll
as my balance wobbles, fails. Time stops, arms
flail above my head. I scrape the ocean bottom.
You reach down, pluck me out. In my eight-
year-old mind you are stronger than the waves.

a thousand tickless moments

The watch you wear: black numbers, gold-rimmed,
with a brown leather band. You always wear it
except when you steer the boat or water-ski
behind it. My job then is to hold it, cradle it,
keep it safe. I hear your heartbeat in each tick.

lying scattered and silent

You and Mom, back together, take me out
for my tenth birthday. I lean into your chest
as we dance across the floor. The swish
of my taffeta dress keeps time to the music.
Everything else disappears in memory's pulse.

nothing left but flights

Twenty years later I fly back to Memphis. You lie
in the polished coffin, stripped of gold cufflinks,
gold watch, and the ring she bought you
to win back your love. I take the watch home,
wear it six days and nights in a row.

into a futureless past

On my birthday that year I'm wearing your watch
as I open my husband's gift: dainty and silver,
with a bracelet band, a fine watch. I burst
into tears, insist it go back to the store. But
the next day I take off your watch, never wear it again.

II. Living the Green Life

Mother's Day Picnic in the Park

We load a basket with mangoes, two kinds of grapes, Brie, Camembert, good ol' Pepperjack, brisket slices from Kansas City Joe's, thermos of OJ, bottle of champagne. The park shimmers in the sunshine like a beached whale, open and empty except for a lone honeybee hovering over the table. After our feast, the others play Frisbee while I pick up trash around the shelter: plastic bottles, bits of charred foil, gum wrappers. I leave the translucent condom where it lies, among the pine needles. A few feet away, by the fence, I see something green: a dollar bill. Then another. Every few feet, blown against the fence line, more money. I picture the scene: late night, girl on top of the picnic table where we just ate, boy on top of her; he reaches into his pocket for a condom. His money drops out, whisked away by the midnight breeze—nine dollars in all. Ah, love.

LGBTQIA and Counting

*We are forced to conclude that human nature is almost
unbelievably malleable . . . .*
　　　　　—Margaret Mead, *Sex and Temperament*

Domain.
　　　　Kingdom.
　　　　　　　Phylum.
　　　　　　　　　　Class.
Order.
　　　　Family.
　　　　　　　Genus.
　　　　　　　　　　Species.

Ranks of order in an ordered world
　　　　or so I thought until I found
　　　　　　　more differences: more colors

than the seven rainbow stripes,
　　　　more tribes than anyone can count.
　　　　　　　And no one can account for

Affinity.
　　　　Attraction.
　　　　　　　Attachment.
Breakdown.
　　　　Breakup.
　　　　　　　Breakaway.
Connection.
　　　　Confusion.
　　　　　　　The ABC's of what it means

to be human. Still digging.
　　　　Discovering. Doing it
　　　　　　　with anything that moves.

Back to the Basics

In watercolor class we make a wheel
with primary colors: red, yellow, blue.
I press the brush into paper, watch edges

spread and contemplate this ancient rite
of making something into something
else. The blank sheet receives red—

world of apples, raspberries, blood.
Yellow blooms next, color of dandelions,
harvest moons, old teeth.

Last, a bold stroke of blue, color of skies,
blood under the skin, indigo buntings—
though they say bird feathers aren't really blue—

something about how light shines when reflected.
Like other things in our universe, mostly illusion.

Queen of Hair

for Jessica

The first thing I noticed was your hair.
Long and thick, it grew through the months
of your first life, silky and soft in womb's air;

then, as things grew cramped, clamped to your head
in inky clumps. When you surfaced, hair first,
into the world's air, with that sleek look of having led

a life in dream-secret places, you resembled a goddess,
hair matted in swirls, curled around your ears.
Meanwhile, back in the sixties, we blessed

and worshipped hair as a way to declare space
for ourselves in a land where hair could grow to
extravagant lengths—they sang its praises

in a Broadway play. Our hippie sisters and brothers
buried pain under shrouds of hair, flown like flags,
crying and raging for all those others

lost to war and death. Now you cry with breath to spare,
shaking your dark crown, claiming your birthright—
freedom's child, Lady Liberty reborn, queen of hair.

At Your Poetry Reading

You talked of growing-up days,
the farm, the freedom, the ordinary

chores that carried you into adulthood—
milk the cow, pluck chickens,

shuck corn, shell peas—simple tasks
that swept the years along like Huck's

raft gliding down that giant river. Your voice
spread its honeyed stories through the room

as those familiar cows and chickens sank
into our listening hearts. We drifted

into that dreamy space created between
what used to be and what might have been

as we walked those plowed rows, gathering
threads of courage to lean into tomorrow.

Untamed

Hail to this messy morning! I rise
early to wander a maze of streets

stunned by sunrise, stroked with gold light
streaking through a silver sky. Housefuls

of garbage slouch at the curb. Weeds poke
through garden mulch. Polka-dot crocuses

frolic through grass gone astray. Shocks
of sorrel and sagebrush, chickweed

and purslane burst into view. I glide by
open windows, spy last night's dishes

dangling in the sink, newspapers strewn
across breakfast tables, no order to this

holy chaos called *life*—cluttered and cupped
with cubbyholes, noisy secrets spilled

from skeletoned closets, unruly
minds, unbordered hearts, scattered wardrobe

of thoughts as blowsy as last week's roses.
I want to shout, make never-before-heard

sounds that launch planets and lure stars, shape
and be shaped by the dream-stuff of night,

intimate shadows of first light. If I
can keep this messy dawn wrapped around me,

I can walk wild all day.

Surrender

There is certainty

in the ocean's path, in the way
waves curl and foam, coming home
to shore before skipping back out,

in the widening spiral of frigate
birds, in the clap and shift
of pelicans' beaks diving

into turquoise waters, and in
the crisp flap of gulls' wings flinging
their way across the horizon.

Can I try for anything less? Why not
call my blood back to beginnings
and aim for the unmasked freedom

of life lived in clear spaces?
Why not fall on my knees, hushed
into openness? If I lean into this cathedral

of clouds and coconut palms bending
in the wind, perhaps I can surrender
to my deepest voice, the one that echoes *yes*

without knowing the questions.

Shore Walk

Between red furrows of dawn
crickets cry light from the shadows.

I wake to the tang of wet sand
slanting down the beach.

Before the day's new barnacles
begin to cling I pause,

read the sea from its edges.
Hills of thick green algae

clumped every few feet.
Water-logged pelican feathers

festooned with snails
and loops of *hijiki,* black seaweed.

Stones smothered with sponges
resting on clam shells

next to bits of coconut husk.
Things piled upon things, tiny shrines

offered to Yemayá, Mother Ocean,
the book of water-life scattering

its spent pages. Tomorrow a new
text will cast its alphabet ashore.

French Quarter Rain Dance

On the corner of Bourbon and Conti
rain cascades from gargoyle

downspouts and slides between
cobblestones. The pale sun escapes

like a disappointed lover. We glide barefoot
with smiles shiny as wet streets, cradled

by thunder and the bright jazz of taxis
cruising by. Why duck under

wrought-iron balconies when it's more fun
to follow the rain and dance in the drops

Bojangles-style? Talk to me, tell me
how when we make love I remind you

of these slick streets, the surprise and splash
of this winsome rain, this dazzling mizzle

where no one wants to stay dry.

The Dream

after a painting by Frida Kahlo

Anchored to death, you still bloomed
toward your future. Your bleached bones—flags

of surrender—broke long ago,
yet your vision never yielded.

You made death your grinning bedmate,
wrapped in timeless bombs ticking

with desire, and grew new roots in your
slumber. You dozed honeyed with yearning,

your vined bed afloat, cloud-surrounded.
Why are your eyes closed? Do you not see?

Even in sleep, your passion stalks the world.

Light Confession

Talk to me about your night
fears. How you keep the light
on beside your bed, hoping

you won't wake and feel
the familiar terror. How you
sleep on your side, turned

away from the window, knowing
they could come through
anyway. How your dreams

are the only things that save you
from your own dread. How ready
you are to plunge into

the undiscovered day,
into whatever
is on the other side of night.

In the Dark

Take away light
and the world grows
larger and smaller—

a whisper travels
down your spine and
saturates the room

a finger's brush
ignites a candle
and a continent

a tongue's flick
ushers your body
through free-falling

space and the inside
of an orchid's
throat—you glide

to the ceiling and dive
into your lungs
where the breath

feels hushed, hidden,
waiting for the tender
graze and final crush

Fifth Season

for Stanley Kunitz

You wrote while tending
your tangled garden
in Provincetown. Your words
thrived among roses,

outlasted peonies, outbloomed
the iris, before you closed your
eyes and filled your mouth
with the silence of forever.

Yet I continue, with the greed
of one who loves flowers and poems
for their essential beauty,
to long for one more season.

Coming Home on the Freeway

At sunset, traffic turns nervous,
    SUV's and blunt-nosed vans
        command the lanes. A red Silverado

darts here and there with the sure grace
    of a dragonfly, stitching lanes together
        as it weaves in and out. The air blooms

with the tang of gasoline, hums with the weary drone
    of tires on asphalt. Behind these wheels sit women
        rehashing the morning's dispute with their lovers

or men hoping they can get home in time
    to have a beer and watch the game. Herds of headlights
        swallow the sun's last rays. As the patter of rain begins,

a thousand windshield wipers twitch and fling it away.
    Lawns have been watered, swimming pools filled. In the suburbs
        rain is nothing but a nuisance. It's already too dark for rainbows.

Bitchin' Truck

She made engine sounds
like oiled whiskey breath
perfumed in blue exhaust

her sleek body bronzed
the color of rainslicked leaves
she had vinyl seats

and a rusted-out bed
that hauled donated sofas
and dressers all over town

she traveled to her own tune
stayed out late and went
wherever she was needed

and she never shuddered
at the roaches and dirty rugs
swept out of rooms

when folks finally moved
into a decent place

In the Garden

Nestled among stones, clusters of webs
shine in the sun, spun across spored fronds

of low-growing fern, woven at crazy-quilt
angles, tilting to the sky like

miniature hammocks, home to tiny
spiders the size of a child's fingernail.

Some webs show ragged holes. Each time
the wind blows they could tear off their frail

moorings and float into uncaring
air. What makes stones sturdy and spider

webs fragile? Where do we humans fit
with our clusters and colonies binged

across the earth's crust, tilting at skies
ragged with ozone holes, basking

in ribbons of bright emissions spun
across the planet? I hear the wind

and wonder with each passing gust
whose house will fall next.

Living the Green Life

Shocking to see these bearded
calves where ice-blank smoothness
met my eyes before. Not since

age twelve were my legs thus
adorned with dark, thick hair
so long it curls upon itself. Why

grow hair now? My friends ask.
It has something to do
with tenderness, I say. These

legs deserve a rest after
almost forty years
of being daily scraped,

sometimes hastily, roughly,
almost always thoughtlessly,
into someone else's idea

of beauty. My neighbor concludes
the same about his lawn: no more
harsh chemicals, grass mowed

to within an inch of its roots.
Let it grow, let it luxuriate
au naturel. My legs, his lawn:

we are about reforestation,
he and I, reclaiming the wild,
preserving the native state of things.

The Language of Graves

has changed. Tombstones engraved with birth and death dates
have long fallen out of favor. Caskets that shouted
satin-lined elegance no longer matter.

Death speaks now from brass urns. Furnaces hiss and translate
their cargo of flesh into glassy smoke rising clouded
through the air. What's left is a whisper, faint rattle

of bone on metal, tattoo of ash that vanishes with the first storm.
For environment's sake, the alphabet of death
becomes simpler still. A shrouded body sinks into green earth

where it welcomes the tongues of nature—murmur of worms
and clicking of beetles transform stilled breath
into dialects of moss and oak, a lexicon of living dirt.

III. Wild Heart

Assignation

She's back. Can't kill her or keep her underground
or freeze her out. She struts forth smiling like the corner

whores, offering hits of pure pleasure in the neon purple
of a crocus nestled next to a rotting fence, in the raw

whistle of blue jays harassing the squirrels, in the pink
whirl of tulip trees gauzy with wind. Spring, you old

mother, you did it again. You lifted your lush green
skirts and made my heart lift in absurd hope. I want

to roll right into your blossomy breasts and suckle
the promise of your pearly air. Later, you'll wash me

in white sun, dress me in your finest forsythia. We'll go
for a quiet stroll before you disappear into hot summer nights.

Plea to the Winter Weather Gods

Boreas, hold back winter's hard grasp,
grass stiff as stone, stones slick with frost,

birds flown to fatter suns. Aeolus, suspend
steel winds that stutter and aim frigid blasts

at unscarved necks. Jupiter, sweep away
skies that court dark more than light,

murky with promise of thunder and sleet.
What shall we sacrifice? Let us refuse

to buy boots; let toes shiver in sandals.
Relegate coats to the closet. Sweet

Eurus, lengthen the days of leaf-cling,
of fall's copper breeze, days when pied light

plays through sycamore trees, teasing
the season's last passion like Psyche herself.

Etude

At twilight I pause to gather crumbs of sunset.
Always, when the sun's last rays scatter into dusk

I feel the gnaw and press of things undone
and you waiting, wanting to be loved. What if

tomorrow the sea suspends its endless cycles,
the sun sleeps, refuses to rise, and you disappear,

memory sunk below heart's horizon, lapping
at blank shores? Then this anxious longing

for less might subside, and I could begin again,
clear as the moon launching its unfettered stride.

Crossing Puget Ridge

I always get lost in Seattle,
surrounded by roundabouts thick
with wild blackberries, hawthorn, ferns,

elderberries, overgrown grasses
and shrubs. My rental car huddles
and circles, tries to decide which spoke

of road to take without falling
into the unknown. Everything shines
wet, luminescent as Oz, but

no landmarks show, no magic road
guides me to my daughter's house
on a dead-end street, one of many

dead-end streets with many roundabouts.
Their names sound familiar, prosaic:
Myrtle, Holly, Willow, Pearl. They might

as well be names of South Sea islands
poking identical heads from the sea.
My daughter's house is a wilderness

of toys, dirty dishes, to-do lists
taped to cabinet doors, the carousel
of spices she scatters into her

stews, the anti-psychotic drugs
she takes to stay sane. Each day I'm here
with her, I pray for direction, hope

for a calming wind, a lessening
of gray, respite from harsh lessons
of uncertain weather, sudden snow

keeping her stranded for hours at work.
Despite help from a smart phone, I'm lost
in this alien place far from home.

I cling to my Midwestern sweater
while everyone else simply throws on
a scarf and a backpack, disappears

down these rabbit hole streets with ease.

New Year's Day in the Coffee Shop

I skate across the brand-new year
still blank, unmarred by harsh words
stirred into the air. The line inside
is silent, smiling, swaying to background
music. A promise of something fresh
lures us all into patience.

As I turn to leave, a toothless man
opens the door, bows with a flourish,
says "Happy New Year." I nod, return
his greeting, and glide forth into a world
gleaming with clean snow. By nightfall
it will have melted into gray slush

and I will have forgotten that we knew
how to be this kind to one another.

A Blessing of Wet Earth

We clear the ground, snow dense and heavy
on our shovels, our humanness never more frail
as we glimpse this thin line arrowing its way
through a vast field of white, our early spring efforts

outlined row by row. To bare this patch one
shovelful at a time may be fools' work but it's also food
for the spirit. Sisyphus, too, claimed joy despite the risk
of angering gods. Laughing, he wouldn't have waited

for an uncertain sun to melt late-winter blues.
The impulse to measure our progress, even in inches, seems
irresistible. Same thing with seeds, no matter
how small: we push them into wet earth and dream

of the summer sustenance, they will become:
melons, cucumbers, squash, peppers, all reaching for the light
even now, even as dusk settles in and cold winds remind us
not to hope for too much this gone-awry spring.

Harvest

With sharp-edged tongues they chopped at the years,
at actions taken or missed, at places where love

failed and hate grew. In the past's matted soil
they rummaged for absolution, dug into the rot

of forgotten slights, deeds gone to seed. Now
everything comes to this—two Venus stalks

tearing at each other in the night, in their dreams,
but in daylight binding themselves side by side,

unyielding, avoiding the desert between them.

Advice to Myself on a Summer Morning

Take nothing for granted.
Thank every fresh-mown lawn
for its irreplaceable scent, every clash
of coffee cups behind the counter as you sit
scribbling as if your life
depended on it—a certain undercurrent
of life, of *duende,* that pulses
next to your blood before tough skin

masks everything. Breathe in
glistening sweetgum leaves, red-tailed
hawks pumping wings as they soar, or sitting
statue-still, and mica-specked pebbles
half-buried in mud. Look for the apertures
(ancestors called them spirit-holes)—
dive into them, take one breath
after another, yield, receive all of it,

all the ordinary sights that make
this life worth wandering through, awake.

Long-Married Love

The anticipation
is not in *if* but *when*,

knowing your touch brings me,
willing, to your body,

yet wondering
if this ripened delight

will still greet us, take us
down passion's green path

until, quiet at last,
we smile at our own creation,

as proud of what we've made
as children with sand castles

that stand tall, flags flying,
before the tides take them.

Training Ground

Buried in crooks and shadows
of the psyche, tribal ghosts

shade the heart (muscle that
inflates and expands

for unknown future losses)
and make room for a banquet

in the darkest recesses
of what some call *soul,*

while old ones whisper
here, have some more

as if there is no end,
no lack, no slackening,

only another measure
of surrender.

Protector

inspired by Elizabeth Darrow's painting, Shaman

In your dreams
you guard the library

of all living things.
You melt the difference

between *past-present-future.*
Time is a nonexistent entity

where no enemy dares trespass
as you enter the holy *kairos*

of *now.* You knit history's
hands into yours

and you shape the world
into your own.

In the green sweep
of your closed-eyed vision

you bring us closer
to that unnameable place

where we all someday
will meet.

After You Died

I relived the years
        over and over
                an old movie drowning
                        in celluloid tears.

I watched us grow
        younger, lighter, less fearful
                until we stood again at the altar
                        heedless of anything

but
love
running
down
our
bodies
like
new
wine.

Spring Training

Smell this gingerbread earth
full of secret seeds—
tulips thrusting up their throats
while a wilderness of love
pushes us out
into the thawing light
where we uncover
the green shoots of honesty
and children chasing fireflies
in the gathering dark—
everything else left behind,
no soldiery or war,
only the endless roar
of a waterfall's edge—
thank god we have more
than one season to get it right.

Lotus

Certain wounds
bloom in the consciousness
forever: white petals floating
in a dark sea,
nourished by decades
of dreams, memories,
darkness layered with darkness,
and still
at the bottom clearly seen—
bright coins of transgressions.

Into my dream he came,
young again.
He knelt at my feet, told me
he wanted to give me something—
a ribbon, a trinket, a jewel—
I knew he looked for a way
to make amends.
I wanted him to know I knew,
in that prescient way
dreams have of shaping us with truth.

I am older
than consciousness itself,
risen to my surface
full of long days and nights—
full of thousands of moons
floating into my life since he first
came—full of darkening seeds
and inescapable wounds.
Taking his hand I invite him
to travel once more

my body's terrain, break open
the seeds of offered grace,
as holy a way to redeem us
as I know. Bowing
to this lifetime's wounded weight,
we have waited long enough
for sorrow's flowering embrace,
for the wafer of regret
to reconstitute itself
as blessing.

Release

When she
was her daughter
she plunged through the layers
from menses to menses
not stopping until the ocean's
bright surface slapped her
she woke in the womb
felt waves immense
surging against her crown

she shook herself
into the world

When she
was her son
she plotted her way
across sunlight
from map to map
until time gapped enough
to slip through
and shave slivers

from roots of *after*
and *before*

When she
came to be only
herself she strapped
the wind to her belly
sliding to the inside
where flying was easy
now she zigzags

her weathervane way
determined not to fade straight
into another life

she wants this one to be the last

Bar Scene

After the third drink bar shadows lengthen,
become lean and tall even if shadowing

less-than-willowy women or portly men.
After the fourth drink the music softens

and drums in the loins as well as the ears,
no tinny-voiced singers, just outroaming lyrics

and hopped-up tunes. After the fifth drink
bar talk is sex talk, full of "what-if's" or "why-not's"

stool by stool. Out on the dance floor her timing
falters but he doesn't notice and pulls her in tighter.

After last call, shadows harden. What's left
of reality vanishes, rosying options

of bedding with strangers rather than sleep
in the harsh-sunned desert of an empty room.

Wild Heart

1.

Wild heart beats—
staccato straws
blown against closed doors
no balance   no balance
in this offbeat world
of rhythm gone awry
no balance no sure-footed
grace   no control
yea though I walk
through the valley
of the shadow of fear
I will not let myself fall

2.

Blue heron beats its wings
in wild grass
lands on one leg
perfectly balanced
bends with grace
to taste the next morsel
I wish for a heron's life
poised   unmoving
one splayed foot
solid as stone

3.

I sleep in the middle
of the bed

walk in the middle
of the valley
open closed doors
cup my beating heart
offer it to the gods
learn to live   unbalanced
on two legs
willing to fall
into whatever is next

Conversation with Jack Kerouac

1.

Believe in the holy contour of life, you said.
And I say *believe in your own holy contour*,
its curves and angles, freckles and frayed ends,

places that stay hidden until they bloom—or burst.
Cattails float above the pond. Their fuzz drifts
everywhere. They're rooted in mud but with heads

lifted, stroked by sky, wind, sun, bronzed and buffeted
in the holy contour of the stream. Moses hidden
in his basket-crib, rocking in the muddy water,

in the sparkle and slime of the river, the same river
that bears us somewhere (anywhere, everywhere)
if we let ourselves float free in time's endless *when*.

2.

Then. Now. Tomorrow. Free and forever, totaled
and summed. But when does a life get totaled?
Whose life did you touch and change forever?

Your road ended too soon but your river still spins
through the mind's landscape, your language
a crucifix, each word sacrificed to the next. That's

the place to stake out the holy contour of what's real,
humming from gutters and rooftops, from bowled bellies
of expectant mothers and their flawed lovers, floating free.

3.

Age three—the war was on, people's lives uprooted,
loosened, changed forever. I sat on a motorcycle nested
between my parents. We rode all over and I felt

safe, danger and beauty existing side by side in my
body, unbroken, free. The beauty and danger of life
lay rooted in my cells. You knew that feeling, too.

It took you all the way to San Francisco and back,
into drugs and sweat and the quest for a Market Street god,
into long paper strips you filled with your mind's thrust.

4.

The thrust of paperwhites, midwinter surprise,
clusters of perfumed white stars clinging to thin green
stalks. The trick is to give them stakes for support

when they need it—before they fall sideways and lose
their fragile charm. A delicate blessing, reminder
to taste the holy contour of each day, let the wild grass

grow without mowing, live without mowing down
hopes, even when they seem as risky
as the fuel spitting from a Harley's pipes. To live

with no thought of tomorrow, you'd say, those biblical
lilies of the field dawning fresh. Free to let death
and the unknown ride with you, and you nested between.

Cutting Trees

The pine beetle
having done its work,
what's left is ours.

We chop down dozens
of lodge pole pines,
hack at thin trunks

until stumps remain.
Silence surrounds us.
No slim shafts

clack in the wind.
No branches
whisper green secrets.

I scan the mountainside.
Thousands of brown trees
lean against living green.

Plenty of pines left. Perhaps
we should save our grief
for what's ahead.

Notes

"Advice to Myself on a Summer Morning" was inspired by Louise Ehrdrich's poem "Advice to Myself." The poem refers to "duende," a Spanish word that Garcia Lorca defined as that passion that "burns the blood like powdered glass."

"Release" relates to the Hindu spiritual concept of *moksha,* freedom or release from the cycle of death and rebirth (samsara).

"Training Ground" was inspired by "The Layers" by Stanley Kunitz.

"Irish Lullaby for the End of the World" was written after attending a concert at Hawks Well Theatre. Brian Finnegan, renowned Irish flute and tin whistle player, closed the concert with a composition in tribute to his mother, whose last name was Starr. The song was titled "The Last of the Starrs" and its haunting melody inspired my poem.

About the Author

Maril Crabtree grew up in Memphis and New Orleans but calls the Midwest home. A former French teacher, lawyer, peace activist, environmentalist, energy healer, and yoga instructor, she is grateful for poetry—hers and others'—as the loom that weaves her life-threads together.

Her most recent chapbook is *Tying the Light* (Finishing Line Press, 2014). She authored two previous chapbooks: *Dancing with Elvis* (Top Hat & Tails Press) and *Moving On* (Pudding House Press), and edited four anthologies of poetry and essays published by Adams Media. A Pushcart Prize nominee, her poetry has won numerous awards, including 1st Place "Judge's Pick" in the anthology *Well-Versed*.

Her work has appeared in numerous journals and anthologies including *Kalliope, I-70 Review, The DMQ Review, Coal City Review, Main Street Rag, Persimmon Tree, Third Wednesday,* and *2014 Poet's Market.* She previously served as poetry editor for *Kansas City Voices* and is a contributing editor for *Heartland! Poems of Love, Resistance & Solidarity.* More of her work can be seen at www.marilcrabtree.com